LONGSIGHT

JILL CRONIN & FRANK RHODES

The History Press

A Whit Walk procession makes its way along New Bank Street in 1955. Members of the Sunday school follow the younger children, who carry flowers and hold on to the ribbons. One of these girls is Diane Brown, holding her mother Sylvia's hand. On the right is a drapery shop with the notice in the window 'Join Our Club'. This was probably for mothers saving all year for new clothes for the Whit Walk.

First published 2010

The History Press
The Mill, Brimscombe Port
Stroud, Gloucestershire, GL5 2QG
www.thehistorypress.co.uk

ISBN 978 0 7524 4655 4

Typesetting and origination by The History Press
Printed in India, Aegean Offset
Manufacturing managed by Jellyfish Print Solutions Ltd

CONTENTS

ACKNOWLEDGEMENTS

We would like to thank all those who have helped us and the people who have given kind permission for us to include their photographs:

Ann Atkinson, Reg Baguley, Dave Cooper, Rosemary Fisher, Pat and Pete Ford, the collection of the late Stan Horritt, Susan Hyde Fielding, Diane Inglis, Ted Kinsey, Dolores Long, Manchester Archives and Local Studies at Central Library, Diane Mercer-Brown, Pat Nicholson, Colin Pemberton, Elsie Slockett, Derek Southall, Gwynne Torr and Richard Wiseman.

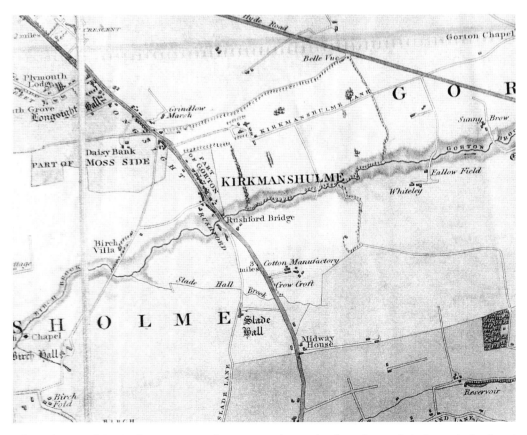

Johnson's map of 1820, showing Longsight as a sparsely populated rural area. Only the main Stockport Road is labelled Longsight, and the Crescent marks the township's boundary with Ardwick. Plymouth Grove joins the main road near Longsight Hall; nowadays its extension emerges near Daisy Bank and Grindlow Marsh. Kirkmanshulme was still then its own area within Newton. The main road continues through Rushford and on to Crowcroft and Midway House, where Levenshulme borders Longsight, on the line of the Nico (or Nicker) Ditch.

INTRODUCTION

Longsight, lying about two miles south-east of the city of Manchester, has complex boundaries: as early as 1871, the magazine *Sphinx* described it as 'a village [that is] situated in a considerable number of townships, which are mixed up with each other in a very remarkable manner'. Longsight fans out like a butterfly from its backbone, Stockport Road, and includes detached areas of Newton (including Kirkmanshulme), Gorton and Moss Side. South lies Levenshulme; west, Rusholme; north, Ardwick; north-west, Chorlton-on-Medlock; and east, Gorton. The Gore Brook bisects Longsight horizontally and the ancient linear earthwork Nico Ditch divides it from Levenshulme.

The name Longsight has various interpretations: 1. 'Long-shut', meaning a shallow, low-lying area; 2. from the long and short sights of a gun kept at the Waggon & Horses public house; 3. the more romantic one that either Bonnie Prince Charlie (resting by the same public house), or the general of the Scottish rebel army (resting by the Red Lion in 1745), remarked, 'What a long sight it is to Manchester!'

Early on, only farming hamlets and scattered cottages existed, such as near Grindlow Marsh, with a few cottages and public houses off the old London Road, near Kirkmanshulme. South lay the village of Rushford, between Rusholme and Slade Hall, with Rushford Bridge crossing the brook. Various street names derive from local landowners: the Siddalls of Slade Hall, the Dean and Canons of the collegiate church in Manchester (later Manchester Cathedral), the Earl of Ducie, and the Anson and Hamilton families.

An Act of 1724 changed the old London Road (following a Roman road) into the Turnpike Stockport Road from Ardwick Green to Buxton, with toll bars by Plymouth Grove West and Slade Lane. Other main routes were Dickenson Road, Slade Lane and Plymouth Grove, which was extended in 1870 to join further south down Stockport Road.

By 1773 there were just 241 houses with a population of 590, rising to 8,511 by 1871. Between 1911 and 1933 the figure rose dramatically to 20,000, but by 2002 had fallen to 16,500. What caused these two booms?

Johnson's map of 1820 shows Longsight as still semi-rural, sparsely populated and with little in the way of industry. There was a small community at Crowcroft around an early cotton mill, on the border with Levenshulme; other than this, the slow-flowing Gore Brook and the lack of canals failed to attract the cotton industry to Longsight.

The coming of the railway in 1836 bisected Longsight; the busy Longsight railway depot and sidings employed many local people for over a hundred years. Longsight station was once Manchester's busiest suburban station, especially for bringing in countless visitors to Belle Vue Zoological Gardens, which straddled both Longsight and Gorton.

The 1830s also saw the creation of Victoria Park, an exclusive housing estate for wealthy Manchester merchants and businessmen – especially for foreign residents. This estate covered parts of Longsight, Rusholme and Chorlton-on-Medlock. Meanwhile, housing was also developing steadily along Stockport and Dickenson Roads and along Stanley and Plymouth Groves.

By the 1870s, the area attracted workers out from the city centre and was packed with terraced housing for the railway, clerical and factory workers, and artisans, with Victoria Park remaining exclusive. Nutsford Vale provided room for engineering, bleach, brick, print and iron works. Brewers, and vinegar and mineral water manufacturers, moved in, plus the vast Daisy Works and the Co-operative printing works. Longsight was amalgamated with the city of Manchester, as was Kirkmanshulme, by the end of the century.

The Longsight entrance to the Belle Vue Zoological Gardens in the early 1900s. The upper storey held a dance floor. This view is taken from inside the gardens. On the right, through the trees, attached to the gateway are houses, where once the elephant keeper Phil Fernandez lived. On the left are more houses, which became the Longsight Inn. The gentleman sitting in the sculpture-filled garden is probably another famous elephant keeper, Lorenzo Lawrence.

Leisure facilities included Belle Vue Zoological Gardens and local theatres and cinemas – the King's, Queen's and Shaftesbury. Longsight Literary and Mechanics' Institute was reborn as Longsight Public Hall and later as the library. Football, cricket, billiards, roller-skating and lacrosse were among the many sports on offer. The Astoria and Grove ballrooms, plus Levenshulme Palais-de-Danse and Belle Vue, provided dancing. Numerous public houses lined Stockport Road.

By the 1930s the area was packed with housing, leaving few open spaces: Crowcroft Park in south Longsight, Grey Street Sand Park in the north and Birch Fields Park on Rusholme's border. Post-war council housing added to the congestion, until the removal of some of the old terraced housing during the mass house clearances in the 1970s.

Longsight welcomed new immigrants from Asia, Ireland and the Commonwealth; Stockport Road, always lined with shops, gained a cosmopolitan atmosphere, with its Asian and Caribbean shops and restaurants. Churches and schools have reflected this cosmopolitan, culturally diverse mix that is Longsight: the Catholic Little Sisters of the Poor and the Catholic Brothers at St Joseph's; Russian, Ukrainian, Church of England, Non-Conformist, and Evangelical, churches; College Methodist and Ivy Independent chapels; the First Church of Christ Scientist; Bethsan Tabernacle; and mosques, all have a place here.

Famous residents have included: the reformer Edwin Chadwick; Sam Wild of the International Brigade; the Jennison family, owners of Belle Vue; Charles Beyer of Beyer Peacock; the painter, Samuel John Lamorna Birch; and the sculptor, John Cassidy, plus many prominent Manchester citizens resident in Victoria Park. The story of Victoria Park is told elsewhere, as it covers Rusholme and Chorlton-on-Medlock as well.

This book tells the varied, rich story of Longsight, through family photographs, early postcards and ephemera. Longsight has welcomed people from all over the world and its history is like a woven, colourful tapestry for its former and newer residents alike, to share and to understand its past, which has created the township as it is today.

Jill Cronin, 2010

ONE

A WALK ALONG STOCKPORT ROAD

The last tram turning off Stockport Road into Slade Lane, on its final journey to the Birchfields Road depot, in 1949 (trams served Manchester from 1901 to 1949). In the middle of the road a policeman directs the traffic, and top right is the Queen's Picture Theatre. The watching crowds stand by the old signpost for Cheadle and the South along Slade Lane, with Stockport directed off to the right.

A sketch by F.L. Tavaré, drawn from a watercolour picture by Daniel Orme, showing Stockport Road at the corner of Longsight Crescent in 1818. By an Act of 1724, the old London Road became the Turnpike Stockport Road, with toll bars, connecting Manchester with Buxton. Here, however, was a private gated toll bar. The Crescent was built in around 1790 by cotton merchant, John Gomm Baker, and later demolished for housing and Kay's Atlas Brewery.

The former Longsight Public Hall and Meeting Rooms on the south-west side of Stockport Road. Opened in 1859 as a Literary and Mechanics' Institute to replace a smaller venue in use from 1855, it included a library, reading room and elementary school, also offering more advanced classes. A galleried hall accommodated concerts, lectures and various entertainments. The Saturday evening readings were particularly popular.

Above: The Hayley Street entrance to the Reading Room at the Longsight Public Hall and Meeting Rooms. As the building became less used, in 1892 it was handed over to Manchester Corporation to become the Longsight Branch Free Library. Proving very successful, it soon had to be enlarged. In 1978 this library closed, when a new one opened on another site on Stockport Road, and it became a community building with a youth centre.

Right: An engraving of Sir Edwin Chadwick, *c.* 1889. Born in Longsight, he became a social reformer and civil servant, pioneering improvements in public health and sanitary conditions. He was Chief Commissioner of the Poor Law Commission in the 1830s and worked with James Kay-Shuttleworth on the first National Board of Health in the 1840s, which culminated in the Public Health Act of 1848.

A blue plaque on a house on Stockport Road, almost opposite Longsight Public Hall. This commemorates Sir Edwin Chadwick, 1800–90, who was born in a cottage on that site and had his first schooling in Longsight. His father, James, was a radical journalist, who must have influenced his son.

Looking north-west along Stockport Road in 1967. Upper Plymouth Grove leads off to the right, where the Plymouth Inn lies on its corner, next to Walter Stamper's butcher's shop. Mark Down's self-service grocery shop is on its other corner, next to the Bengal restaurant, with the Westmoreland Arms further up. Plymouth Grove West leads off left with a chemist's on its far corner and a boot and shoe shop on its near corner.

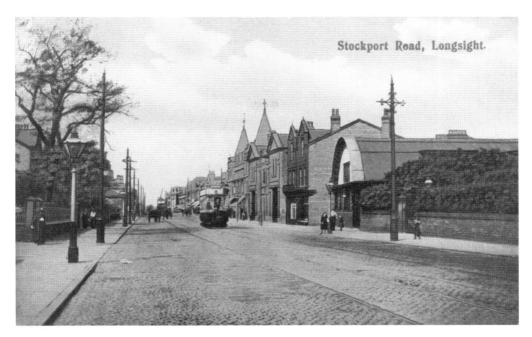

Looking north-west along Stockport Road in 1907. On the right is probably a Temperance billiards hall with its curved roof. North of it lay the Manchester & Withington Imperial steam laundry. Daisy Works Mill would later be extended over that area.

Looking north along Stockport Road in 1910. On the right is Longsight Wesleyan Methodist Chapel. Two large houses with big gardens stand next to it. Later, Pownall's Daisy Works Mill would be built over them.

The north-east side of Stockport Road, with a tram bound for Albert Square turning into Plymouth Grove, in 1947. From the left are a laundry and the butcher's department of the Manchester & Salford Equitable Co-operative Society, with a fine mosaic logo along the base of the shop window. Next comes a dyer's and cleaner's next to a bookseller-cum-stationer, near the corner of Newton Avenue.

A view of the south-west side of Stockport Road in the early 1900s. Birch Lane leads off right, just past the Waggon & Horses public house. This is the earlier building that housed the pub, with Oglee, a dentist's, next door. Next is C. Howarth, a dealer in hay, straw and corn, and then Ogden's general store.

The original part of Overton House on Newton Avenue, just off Stockport Road, near Kirkmanshulme Lane. Overton House or Lodge, with its stables and well, dates back to at least 1830, when, named Rose Cottage, Thomas Knight and Joseph Higginbottom held its lease. In 1850 it passed from Whitmore Henry Perkes to Martha Mary Lay and then in 1855 to John Leigh.

Overton House, with its later extension on the right, c. 1969. John Leigh carried out improvements, adding a bathroom, scullery and pantry, and then let it to Dr Joseph Gibson Dowses, the first of many doctors there. Dr Conway bought it in around 1892, and added the section nearer to Stockport Road in 1903. Other doctors followed and now it is a residential home. Its stables were once used by the Waggon & Horses public house across the road. (Courtesy of Manchester Archives and Local Studies at Central Library)

Stockport Road, with Kirkmanshulme Lane leading off on the left, in the 1960s. The Royal Oak public house stood for many years on the corner of the lane. Here a fine building houses various shops: from the left, Allison's outfitters; Samuel Oswald house furnisher; Dress-U-Well; Direct Fish Supplies Ltd and a grocery. Poultry is hanging up outside the fish shop, as quite often fish and poultry were sold together. (Courtesy of Manchester Archives and Local Studies at Central Library)

Opposite, above: Yew Tree cottages on the north-east side of Stockport Road in the early 1900s. These were demolished in 1904 to make way for the King's Opera House. Two of the cottages on the left are shops and one on the right has a 'For Sale' sign. Groups of children stand outside the shops, one of which advertises that 'Lyon's Ink Never Fades'.

Opposite, below: A view of the north-east side of Stockport Road in the 1970s. On the right is the building which once housed the King's Opera House, used as a theatre and later as a cinema. The tower is missing its clock. Once its integral shops included 'the King's Picture Post Card' shop, a tobacconist, newsagent and confectioner. Shepley Street leads off on the right. (Courtesy of Manchester Archives and Local Studies at Central Library)

A view of the north-east side of Stockport Road in the 1960s. The clock was still in place at that time, on the King's Opera House on the left. The double-fronted shop is Allendale & Allendale's greengrocery. Next door, the signboard belongs to the Church Hotel, which is set back from the road. Two doors along lies the Longsight Tavern. (Courtesy of Manchester Archives and Local Studies at Central Library)

Looking south-east along Stockport Road in the early 1900s. On the near left, Mundy (later Motherwell) Street, leads off beside the Coach & Horses Hotel (landlord William Mundy). The row ends at the corner of Stanley Grove; across the road stands a branch of the grocer T. Seymour Mead & Co. On the right-hand side of Stockport Road were boot and shoe shops, the UCP café, a grocery, and a branch of William Deacon's bank on the corner of Dickenson Road.

Above: A closer view of the Stanley Grove and Stockport Road junction in 1906. On the left-hand corner is a dispensary (later a boot and shoe shop), next to Whitham's shop, which would become the Argenta Meat Co. by 1913. On the right-hand corner is the large establishment of the grocery chain T. Seymour Mead & Co., plus a butcher's shop, tripe dealer, fruiterer and stationery shop on the corner of Spring Gardens.

Right: Herbert Hanbury Smith-Carington, who lived on Stanley Grove, in 1899. Originally from Worcester, he moved to Longsight in 1874 as assistant secretary to Sir Joseph Whitworth & Co. Ltd, and became a director in 1887, later becoming director of the new company Sir W.G. Armstrong, Whitworth & Co. Ltd. He was a member of many local societies and chairman of the Manchester Southern Hospital for women and children and Manchester Maternity Hospital. He also served on the committee for the Manchester Steam Users' Association.

Looking down Stanley Grove from Stockport Road in the early 1900s. On the left corner is the chemist's cash dispensary shop, with Stanley Hall above it, advertising Sunday school at 2 p.m. On the right-hand corner is the grocery of T. Seymour Mead & Co., with the premises of the Longsight Conservative Club above it.

Opposite, above: A sketch, by F.L. Tavaré, of the toll bars across both Stockport Road and Slade Lane in the early 1900s. In between stands a toll house, a relic of the days when Stockport Road was the turnpike road from Manchester to Buxton. The former London Road, leading out from Ardwick Green along Roman lines, was upgraded to this main thoroughfare by an Act of 1724. The railway bridge of the former Manchester to Birmingham Railway crosses over Stockport Road on the left.

Opposite, below: An early view of the corner of Dickenson and Stockport Roads in the early 1900s. The two policemen seem to be posing for the photograph. On Dickenson Road (on the left) are numerous advertisements for: Compo, Seymour Mead's tea, Whitbread's stout for *2s 6d*, Deakin's, Yorkshire Relish and the Hippodrome and Empire. The old houses along Stockport Road, with steps up to their front doors, appear derelict.

The junction of Stockport Road, with Slade Lane on the right, in the early 1900s. Between the two roads lies a toll house. Long after the tolls were abolished, the buildings were demolished in around 1934 to improve visibility for road users. A variety of horse-drawn delivery carts and wagons travel along the roads over the tram lines: the then familiar tram sign on the left-hand post reads 'All cars stop here'. In the distance is the railway bridge.

A view of the north-east side of Stockport Road, where nearby Slade Lane leads off to the left, in 1958. The Queen's Picture Theatre is on the far left, in those days owned by Cinema Manchester Ltd. Next come the Crown garage and hotel, set back from the main road. A newsagent's follows, then Rushford Terrace, a hairdresser's shop and a tobacconist. The Rolling Stones are said to have stopped at the newsagent's shop in a vain bid to buy a copy of the *New Musical Express*, when they had a hit record. (Courtesy of Manchester Archives and Local Studies at Central Library)

Above: Another view of the Slade Lane and Stockport Road junction in 1924. The array of shops and people on the right-hand side shows the busy nature of Stockport Road. The shops include the telegraph office (near right).

Left: The old boundary signpost of the London & North Western Railway – near the railway bridge over Stockport Road, across from its junction with Slade Lane.

The rebuilding of the Stockport Road/Slade Lane railway bridge in the late 1950s. This was for the electrification of the railway; in the late nineteenth century the bridge had already been widened to allow more road traffic. It carried the trains of the former Manchester to Birmingham railway company. The left-hand walls have advertisements for wrestling at Belle Vue Zoological Gardens, Wall's ice cream, the Hippodrome, McEwan's export ale and the Wakes Week fair.

Left: An early metal milestone under the railway bridge on Stockport Road, near Slade Lane. It reads, 'To St Ann's Square three miles' and has Manchester City's coat of arms at the top. Some of these posts were removed for the war effort in 1939.

Below: The small police station on Stockport Road outside Crowcroft Park, *c.* 1959. The building is still there but is used as business offices. There were also two police houses on a small croft on the North Road side of the park. The main Longsight police station was in North Longsight in the former St Joseph's Industrial School, near the border with Ardwick. (Courtesy of Manchester Archives and Local Studies at Central Library)

TWO

PEOPLE AND PLACES

From left to right: Pat, Denise Roberts, Andrena and Janet pose near their homes in Longsight in the late 1950s. The maze of terrace housing, which included their homes, would later be cleared away in the 1970s to make way for more modern housing with new street names.

A view along Anson Road in 1909. It is difficult to equate this quiet, deserted scene with the bustling road of today. It is named after the Anson family, who lived at Birch Hall (now the site of Manchester Grammar School). Anson Road was on the edge of the elite Victoria Park housing estate and had toll gates. The volume of traffic, including trams, forced the abolition of the tolls in 1938 and opened up the road.

A view along Birch Hall Lane in 1909. A lone figure, possibly a gardener, stands in the road. This lane once led to Birch Hall and its farm and thirty-acre estate. The Birch family owned all this until 1743. In 1888 Birch Fields Park was created on the estate, and in 1926 the hall was demolished.

Right: A blue plaque on the wall of No. 57 Birch Hall Lane. It commemorates Sam Wild, who became a commander of the British Battalion in the International Brigade and fought in the Spanish Civil War of 1936–39. Born in Ardwick, he lived at this house in Longsight from 1940–59.

Below: Sam Wild on the left with a colleague, Bob Cooney, in Spain, *c.* 1936. Sam won the Spanish Medal of Valour for his efforts: as the last commander of the British Battalion he fought, despite being injured, until forced to give up his weapons. His wife raised money and sent food and aid to the troops and his daughter Dolores is named after Dolores Ibarruri, a revolutionary leader who personally thanked the International Brigade.

Above: Sam Wild with his friends and colleagues in Spain, *c.* 1936. From the left, back row: Ted Edwards, Sam Wild and Peter Kerrigan. Front row: George Fletcher, Paddy O'Daire, Alan Gilchrist and Bob Cooney. About sixty-six Manchester men travelled to Spain to join the International Brigade to fight against the rise of General Franco's Fascists. The year 2008 was the seventieth anniversary of the defeat of the Republican forces in the Spanish Civil War.

Left: The imposing front of the former German Consulate, on Birch Lane in 2001, after its transformation into the Bangladeshi community centre. The German eagle perches high above the entrance, the ornate mouldings and the balconied first-floor window. Once a revolving door graced that entrance. Many German merchants lived in Victoria Park, part of a large community across Rusholme, Longsight and Greenheys.

Birch Lane, *c.* 1920. Named after the Birch family, this lane was separated from Birch Hall Lane by Dickenson Road. John Dickinson owned the Birch Hall estate from about 1745: his mother was a member of the Birch family.

A view looking south-west along Dickenson Road in 1906. Although named after John Dickinson, the road is usually spelled Dickenson. Birch Hall Lane leads off left and Birch Lane right, where a lamppost is set on a triangular piece of ground. Tree-lined garden walls stretch ahead. Draycote House with its large garden lies on the corner of Birch Hall Lane.

A view looking north-east along Dickenson Road in 1909. The same lamppost stands on its triangle of land on the left, on the corner of Birch Lane. Opposite, both Beresford Road and Birch Hall Lane lead off, where the two men are standing. Near them is possibly a postman with his horse-drawn van further down the road.

William Brown in his mother Sylvia's arms, on Ernest Street, in 1948. It was a short street north of Richmond Grove East, running from Morton Street to New Bank Street, which ran parallel with the railway lines. These terraced houses would be swept away for a new housing estate.

Sandra Hampson races along Elgar Street in 1974. Behind her in the background is Pink Bank Lane with William Ayrton's works. Elgar Street lies between Pink Bank Lane and Northmoor (formerly North) Road.

The junction of High Street (later Hathersage Road) and Upper Brook Street, in 1908. Only the east end of High Street forms Longsight's border with Chorlton-on-Medlock. High Street leads off Plymouth Grove down to Oxford Road. A hansom cab, tram, and bike share the roadway. On the left is an open space, beyond which Blackstake Farm used to stand.

Looking east along Kirkmanshulme Lane from Stockport Road in 1907. Kirkmanshulme was a separate entity lying in Longsight. The railway bridge in the distance is by Longsight station. On the right lies the Royal Oak public house, then a Threlfall's brewery house, with 'Belle Vue Gardens' inscribed over its doorway.

Looking east along Kirkmanshulme Lane, towards an entrance to Belle Vue Zoological Gardens off on the left, in 1916. On the right is the gateway to Willow Bank House near Albert Grove; other houses stretch along the lane to the turning into North Road, opposite the woman in the distance. On the left is the wall of Kirkmanshulme House with its extensive gardens.

Above: One of the lanes leading to Belle Vue Zoological Gardens, off Kirkmanshulme Lane, 1906. In the distance is the Longsight entrance gateway. Longsight station is nearby, off to the left. A cricket ground, and the row of houses known as Tank Row, also lie off to the left; the people are probably watching a cricket match.

Right: John Jennison, grandson of John Jennison the founder of Belle Vue Zoological Gardens, in 1899. Son of Richard, one of John's many children who helped to run Belle Vue, he lived at the Lodge (now demolished). Born at Belle Vue in 1867, he became an architect, designing the Empress ballroom at Blackpool, the piers and Winter Gardens at Morecambe, the pier at Colwyn Bay and both Haydock and Chester racecourses.

Left: 'Sunny' Lowry as a young swimmer. Sunny, real name Ethel, was born in 1911 and lived on Kirkmanshulme Lane; she was second cousin to the artist L.S. Lowry. Sunny swam at Victoria Baths on Hathersage Road and in 1933 made the record books on her successful third attempt to swim the English Channel. She was awarded the MBE and held various offices in sport. Sunny lived to see Victoria Baths win money for restoration work, with her backing, and died aged ninety-seven in 2008.

Below: A group of Georgian houses near Longsight railway station and depot in 1988. They lay near Tank Row.

Another view of the houses near Longsight railway station in 1988. By the early 1990s they were derelict, and were later demolished in 1995.

Lillian Brindley with her young daughter Gillian, and her neighbours, outside her home on Link Street in the 1950s.

Above: Lillian Brindley with her daughter Gillian standing on Link Street in the 1950s. Dalby Street is in the background and Link Street joined Mitton Street at its other end. These streets ran between Kirkmanshulme Lane and Stanley Grove and were demolished in the house clearances. The railway runs along left, parallel with Link Street.

Left: Beryl Nicholson near her home on Morton Street in 1953. Wearing her 'Sunday best', she is ready for the Whit Walks. Behind her, Florence Street turns off to the left: it ran between Morton and New Bank Streets.

Gwynne Brindley standing on Link
Street in 1967.

Lillian Brindley standing on Link Street
in the 1950s.

A 1933 advertisement for F. Annable & Son, builders and contractors of West Gorton. Their housing estates are found in various towns, usually with one road named Annable. Here they are advertising their new houses on the North (later Northmoor) Road estate. Their description of the local area, and of the layout and contents of these houses, is glowing. The inclusion of an outside coal-house, cooking range, bathroom and separate toilet, plus a garage site and garden, would be quite a luxury in the 1930s.

Opposite, above: A plan of the 1840s, showing where Plymouth Grove once joined Stockport Road. Originally Plymouth Grove turned to meet Stockport Road where Plymouth Grove West now runs. In 1870 it was extended to meet Stockport Road in its present position and the gates to Victoria Park were moved back to Daisy Bank Road. Large houses such as Longsight Abbey, Longsight Hall, Plymouth Grove House, Plymouth Lodge and Grindlow House once adorned this area.

Opposite, below: A view along Plymouth Grove in Edwardian times. Here the area still appears tree-lined and fairly traffic-free but the tram lines show how the area was being opened up.

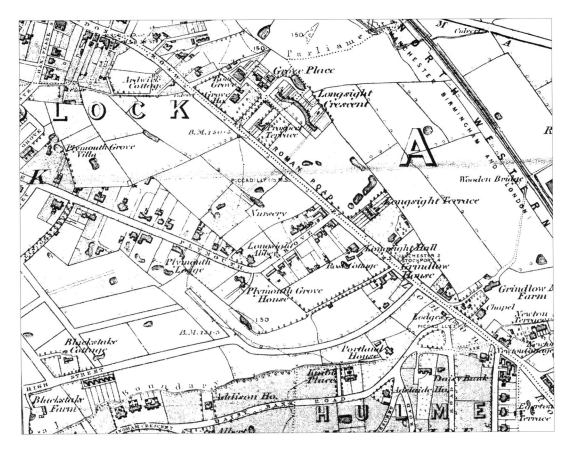

A view along Plymouth Grove in the early 1900s. This once fashionable road was graced by large houses, occupied by such people as Elizabeth and William Gaskell. On the right are the gates and toll house at the entrance to the select housing estate, Victoria Park, where many rich, often foreign, merchants lived in large houses with extensive grounds. The population spread steadily out from Manchester city and later the secluded area of Victoria Park found itself under pressure from traffic and cheaper housing.

Opposite, above: A view along Plymouth Grove in the early 1900s. This road lay partly in Chorlton-on-Medlock and partly in Longsight. High Street (later Hathersage Road) was the border on one side, but Longsight did not begin until Richmond Grove on the north side of the road.

Opposite, below: Hulme Hall on the south side of Plymouth Grove in 1910. This was a hall of residence for Owens College, which would become the Victoria University of Manchester and grow and grow to its present size. The hall lay just near the border of Longsight with Chorlton-on-Medlock. Avenue House lay to the west of Hulme Hall and on the right were the houses on Alexandra Grove. By the 1930s the college was gone and smaller houses and shops covered its site.

Plymouth Grove, Longsight

Hulme Hall, Manchester

Richmond House, now known as Grove Park House, on the east side of Plymouth Grove West. The gateposts still bear its original name. This was a private house, lived in by a doctor in the 1950s.

Left: One of the gateposts to Portland Crescent. The crescent curves round from High Street (later Hathersage Road) to end at Plymouth Grove by St Joseph's Roman Catholic Church. Portland House and garden once lay here on the edge of Victoria Park. The presbytery of St Joseph's Church has been on this crescent for some years.

Opposite, above: The exterior of No. 25 Portland Crescent, known as 'The Hut'. In the 1870s William Flynn, a buyer, lived at No. 25 in a row called Drayton Villas. This house has fine stained-glass windows of the early 1900s. By 1930 an architect called William Ellerton occupied this house through to the 1950s, as the firm of architects called Graves & Ellerton.

Opposite, below: Slade Hall, off Slade Lane on the border of Longsight and Levenshulme, in 1908. The estate also lay in Gorton and Rusholme and dates back to the 1200s. A Manchester family lived there and they adopted the name of Slade. In the 1580s the Siddalls (Syddalls) were in residence there. This timber-framed building was erected in the sixteenth century, with various additions and alterations made over the years.

Richmond Grove, viewed from Victoria Road in the early 1900s. The road runs between High Street (later Hathersage Road) and Stockport Road. On the left are three-storey houses, one of which is marked by two crosses. On the back of the postcard is an interior plan of this house plus the description: 'water gramma outside, six bedrooms & little boxroom. Little, wee garden could be made quite nice. The smaller bedrooms are all much better than any of the others we have seen.'

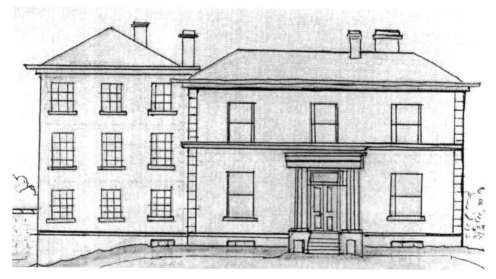

A sketch of the home of Charles Frederick Beyer (1813–76) on Stanley Grove in the late 1800s. He lived in this fine house with its twenty-five rooms, which included eight bedrooms; one bathroom; breakfast, dining and drawing rooms; a library and a beer cellar. Charles Beyer was a partner in the firm of Beyer & Peacock, which designed and built steam trains in Gorton. He funded the building of St Mark's Church and rectory in West Gorton, the rebuild of St James's Church, and the building of All Saints' Church in Gorton.

THREE

OUT OF DOORS

The Brown family enjoy a day out in Crowcroft Park in 1953. Diane sits in front of her maternal grandmother, Mary Shaw. Her brother Bill sits behind her other brother, Steve. The family lived in Longsight, first at Ernest Street near Richmond Grove East and then on East Road from around 1954.

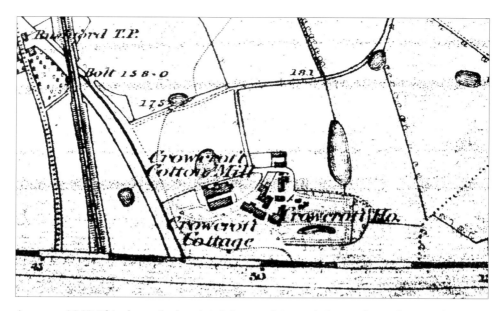

A map, *c.* 1840. This shows the hamlet of Crowcroft in south Longsight, to the east of Stockport Road, where today Crowcroft Park touches the border of Levenshulme. Originally Crowcroft was home to Crowcroft Cottage, house, farm and cotton mill. Cotton mills were rare in Longsight but this one existed in the 1820s until around the mid-nineteenth century. Previously, Thomas Knight of Crowcroft employed hand-loom weavers.

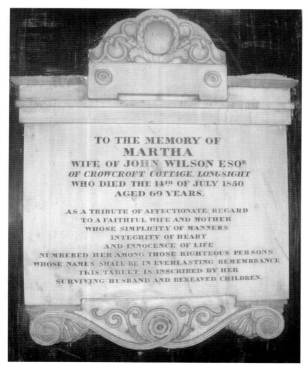

TO THE MEMORY OF
MARTHA
WIFE OF JOHN WILSON ESQ.
OF CROWCROFT COTTAGE, LONGSIGHT
WHO DIED THE 14TH OF JULY 1850
AGED 69 YEARS.

AS A TRIBUTE OF AFFECTIONATE REGARD
TO A FAITHFUL WIFE AND MOTHER
WHOSE SIMPLICITY OF MANNERS
INTEGRITY OF HEART
AND INNOCENCE OF LIFE
NUMBERED HER AMONG THOSE RIGHTEOUS PERSONS
WHOSE NAMES SHALL BE IN EVERLASTING REMEMBRANCE
THIS TABLET IS INSCRIBED BY HER
SURVIVING HUSBAND AND BEREAVED CHILDREN.

Left: A memorial tablet inside Brookfield Unitarian Church in Gorton. The original Gorton chapel served a wide area. Here the tablet is in memory of Martha Wilson, who lived with her husband John in Crowcroft Cottage and died in 1850. In the 1870s Patrick Crane Moir, an oil merchant, lived there, while Mrs Mary Aitken occupied Crowcroft House and Mr R. Melling farmed Crowcroft Farm. In 1919, Henry Norburn, the first rector of St Agnes's Church, lived at Crowcroft House.

Opposite, below: A view of Crowcroft Park in the early 1900s. When Crowcroft Park was opened in 1900 it covered fourteen acres, and fifteen more were added in 1926.

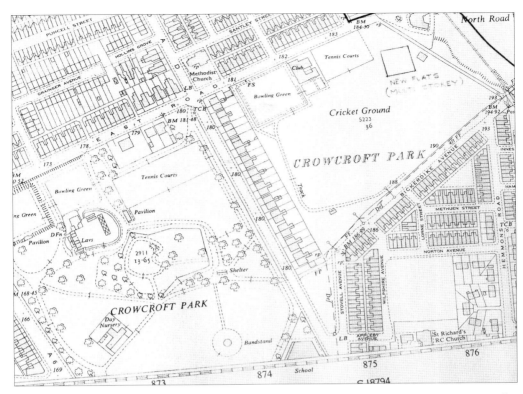

Above: A plan of Crowcroft Park in 1952, showing how the park was landscaped with lawns, paths, trees and flowerbeds. Its amenities included: three bowling greens with club house, four tennis courts, two pavilions, a rest shelter, public conveniences, a bandstand and several cricket – and later football – grounds. The cricket ground has long been home to Longsight cricket club.

Another view of a tree-lined path in Crowcroft Park, 1914.

Crowcroft Park in 1915. The park is bounded by East Road on its north side, North (later Northmoor) Road on the east and Stockport Road on the west side, with entrances from both Longsight and Levenshulme. Housing on North Road can be seen through the trees.

Families enjoy a day out in Crowcroft Park in 1914. In the distance is the bandstand with the houses of North Road behind it. The Victorian bandstand has gone now. North of it was an 'elderly men's rest shelter': a summer shed with an open side, with the roof supported by tree trunk columns set on stone bases. Both lay in the south-east corner of the park, near the border with Levenshulme.

The Terrace in Crowcroft Park, 1911. Children in their 'Sunday best' are on the terrace walk in front of the well-kept sloping beds, which overlook a bowling green. Steps lead up to the top bowling green, where one of the original buildings, Crowcroft House, still survives today with its stable block behind it. It became the park keeper's home. The houses in the background are on North Road as it curves round the park.

The former stable block inside Crowcroft Park, which lies behind the house and the top bowling green, and now houses offices for the park staff. The park had deteriorated by the end of the twentieth century but the Friends of Crowcroft Park achieved regeneration and in 2000 their young helpers were awarded the Philip Lawrence prize (for young people who make a positive impact in the community). A children's playground has been established in the north-east corner.

Sylvia and Bill Brown in Crowcroft Park with their daughter Diane, *c.* 1960. Behind them to the right lie Crowcroft Park infants' school in Longsight and housing on North Road.

Above: Stuart (on the left) and Steve Brown stand with park keeper Stan in Crowcroft Park, near Stockport Road, in the early 1960s. Other open spaces are nearby Matthews Lane Quarry (landscaped as an open amenity) and a small recreation ground at Grey Street in north Longsight, on its border with Ardwick. Also known as the Sand Park, the latter utilised a former tram-shed stable (for horses of the Manchester Carriage & Tramways Co.) as an all-weather shed for the park.

Right: Carol Brown, daughter of Steve and Janet Brown, and Sandra Hampson (on the right) enjoy the children's roundabout in Crowcroft Park in the early 1970s.

Left: Children enjoying the open air at Stanley Grove day nursery in the early 1970s. At the back, second from the right, stands Sandra Hampson, with Susan Higginbottom on her right. Crowcroft Park day nursery was placed at the south-west corner of the park and Crowcroft Park Primary School also lies on its south side.

Below: The north-east lodge and Longsight entrance to Birch Fields Park in the early 1900s. Most of Birch Fields Park lies in Rusholme, but this gate gives access for Longsight residents off Dickenson Road. Opened in 1888, the park covers the estate of Birch Hall. The hall itself was demolished in 1926 to make way for Manchester Grammar School. The park is bisected by the Gore Brook and was provided with sports areas and a bandstand.

FOUR

WORK AND SHOPS

The name-plate above the entrance to the Assembly Hall of the Beswick Co-operative building, on North (later Northmoor) Road. This magnificent building has been listed and restored to its former architectural glory as it first looked in 1912. This was part of the 1998 Northmoor renewal area, when the building was converted into flats and a community centre. The pavement outside is inlaid with cast bronze artwork of poems by young people.

An open day at Longsight depot in 1990, with engines in steam. Longsight's first short-lived station in 1840 was a halt at Rushford Bridge, near Slade Lane bridge: it closed when Longsight station was opened here, off Kirkmanshulme Lane, in 1842. Longsight provided one long bay 'excursion platform' for day-trippers to nearby Belle Vue. Once one of Manchester's busiest suburban stations, it served the Manchester to Birmingham (later the London & North Western) Railway, closing in 1958 after over a hundred years of use.

Opposite, above: A map of the 1840s showing Longsight carriage and engineering depot just north of the station. Opened in 1840 by the Manchester to Birmingham railway company, this depot had the oldest surviving locomotive shed in the country. Here was an original hexagonal round house with a turntable for the engines. It was later demolished and replaced by a straight shed lying alongside the railway lines.

Opposite, below: A map of 1915 showing the later carriage and engine sheds at the Longsight depot. The sheds are surrounded by the complex Longsight sidings, which developed to cater for the busy traffic from Manchester's London Road station. Once 200 locomotives could be housed here, and there were additional sidings for Belle Vue traffic. Many Longsight people had employment here. Housing at Tank Row lay nearby on the right. A reservoir for a water supply, and the station itself, lie off to the right.

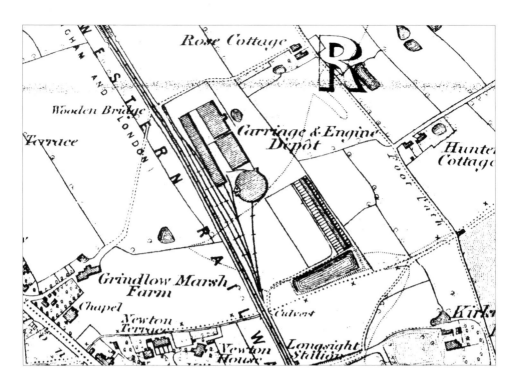

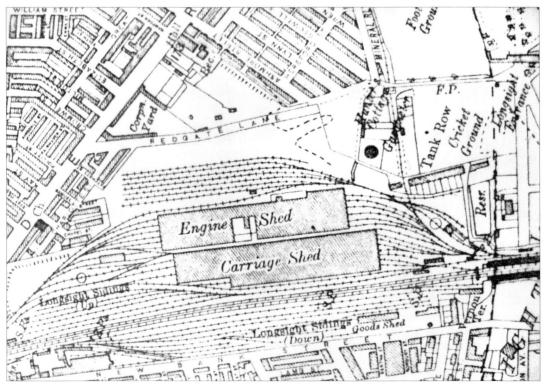

A customer account card for Ridings Stores Ltd, covering the years 1954–6. Riding Stores Ltd had branches in Chorlton-in-Medlock, Rusholme, Gorton and Lower Openshaw, plus other areas. Their branch at Longsight was on Richmond Grove East, selling a variety of electrical household goods, furniture, clothing, carpets, baby goods, radios and cycles. The customer paid an agreed weekly amount and it was all recorded on this card.

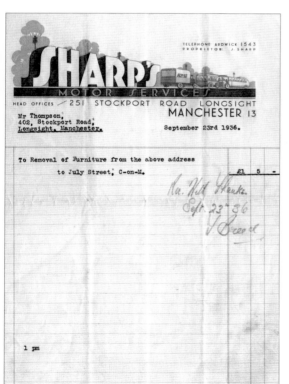

Left: The billhead of Sharp's Motor Services, on Stockport Road, for 1936. Jack Sharp was a motor coach proprietor based next to the Co-operative society stores near Halsbury Street. His business was there in the 1920s and continued through the 1950s at that site. Jack had wagons (for removals) and coaches (for outings).

Opposite, above: An advertisement for Manchester Garages on Kirkmanshulme Lane in the 1960s. Their Greyhound service station provided petrol as well as selling used cars. This tradition of car sales has continued around the former site of Belle Vue Zoological Gardens, especially along Hyde Road.

Opposite, below: The main store of the Beswick Co-operative Society in Longsight on Northmoor (formerly North) Road. The architecture is inspiring and the tower of this building is guarded by carved birds, as was their building on Slade Lane. The Beswick Society also had smaller branches on Stockport Road and on side streets. The Manchester and Salford Equitable Co-operative Society had various branches along Stockport Road, including a pharmacy, butcher's and grocery.

Opposite, above: The front of the Co-operative building on North Road housed various types of shops. This is a rare survivor of the mosaic entrance to one of the shops, bearing the initials of the society.

Opposite, below: The Slade Lane branch of the Beswick Co-operative Society, just before it was revamped in 2006. The fine decoration on the roof included a bronze decorative frieze and the figures of various birds, including this large eagle. The building lies near the corner of Slade Lane and Stockport Road, between Slade Grove and Portland Road.

The membership card of Doris Young, showing the 'divi' (dividend) she earned by shopping at the Slade Lane Co-operative Society between the years 1955 and 1970. In its early days, Nos 2–6 housed the Beswick Society with a grocery and other departments, while Nos 10–12 housed the Manchester and Salford Equitable Co-operative Society. In between, No. 8 was Stenton Glider cycle works. By the 1940s the Beswick Society ran the whole building from Nos 2–12.

A drawing of the extensive Co-operative Wholesale Society Ltd printing works, on the corner of Hamilton and Stamford Roads. It was opened in July 1898. The right-hand section was demolished in around 1970 and the works were closed down in July 1970. Some buildings still remain.

A view of the former Co-operative Wholesale Society Ltd printing works on Hamilton Road in 2006. This was a vast complex, bounded by Rainford Street and Stamford, Hamilton and Dickenson Roads. There was a similar Co-operative Society printing works nearby in South Reddish.

A view of the former Valpercy works on Stamford Road in 2006. William Percival & Co. produced high quality ladies' underwear. The vast frontage stretches along Stamford Road and the building is also bounded by Albert Place and Hamilton Road.

Established 1882   Telephone : Rusholme 13

ON TIME

LONGSIGHT LAUNDRY

Rainforth Street, LONGSIGHT

HIGH-CLASS WORK

Collections and Deliveries in the City, Weaste, Bramhall, Cheadle, Cheadle Hulme, Davenport, and all the Southern Suburbs

PROPRIETORS : CHORLTON & HUMPHREYS
(J. Chorlton, H. Humphreys)

A 1929 advertisement for the Longsight Laundry on Rainforth Street. This laundry lay between Dickenson and Stamford Roads. Operating from 1882, it provided a service for homes without washing machines, when towels and bedding were difficult to manage at home. It collected and delivered to a wide area of the suburbs and towns south of the city centre and claimed high-class work.

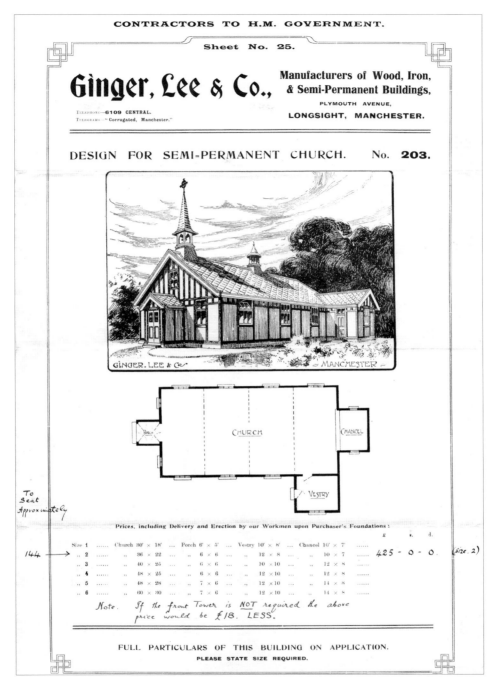

Sheet No. 25.

Ginger, Lee & Co.,

Manufacturers of Wood, Iron, & Semi-Permanent Buildings,

PLYMOUTH AVENUE,

LONGSIGHT, MANCHESTER.

TELEPHONE—**6109 CENTRAL.**
TELEGRAMS—"Corrugated, Manchester."

DESIGN FOR SEMI-PERMANENT CHURCH. No. **203.**

To Seat Approximately

144

Prices, including Delivery and Erection by our Workmen upon Purchaser's Foundations :

								£	s.	d.
Size 1	......	Church 30′ × 18′	...	Porch 6′ × 5′	...	Vestry 10′ × 8′	... Chancel 10′ × 7′	......		
,, 2	......	,, 36 × 22	...	,, 6 × 6	...	,, 12 × 8	... ,, 10 × 7	425 - 0 - 0. (size. 2)		
,, 3	......	,, 40 × 25	...	,, 6 × 6	...	,, 10 × 10	... ,, 12 × 8	......		
,, 4	......	,, 48 × 25	...	,, 6 × 6	...	,, 12 × 10	... ,, 12 × 8	......		
,, 5	......	,, 48 × 28	...	,, 7 × 6	...	,, 12 × 10	... ,, 14 × 8	......		
,, 6	......	,, 60 × 30	...	,, 7 × 6	...	,, 12 × 10	... ,, 14 × 8	......		

Note. If the front Tower is NOT required the above price would be £18. LESS.

FULL PARTICULARS OF THIS BUILDING ON APPLICATION.

PLEASE STATE SIZE REQUIRED.

A design by Ginger, Lee & Co. for a semi-permanent church in Manchester, in the late 1940s. This company produced sectional buildings and were contractors to the government: buildings like this would be needed post-war to replace war-damaged structures. The business moved to Plymouth Avenue, after starting out in a joiner's timber yard on Morton Street in the early 1900s, but by the 1960s they had transferred to Hamilton Road.

ESTABLISHED
TO BREWE YE GOODE OLDE ALE.
ATLAS BREWERY.
JAMES KAY,
STOCKPORT-ROAD, MANCHESTER.
PURE MALT AND HOP ALES
FOR FAMILY USE.

Nine and 18 Gallon Casks, 1s. per gallon, recommended.
May be tasted and orders given: BREWERY and
56, CORPORATION-STREET, CITY.
These ALES, and NO OTHERS, SOLD at the SPREAD
EAGLE VAULT, opposite Corn Exchange, Hanging Ditch.

Opposite, above: A newspaper advertisement for James Kay's ales in 1881. His Atlas Brewery lay on Stockport Road near Grey Street, on the border of Longsight and Ardwick. In 1878 Hannay & Dickson traded from there as wine and spirit merchants but, in the early 1880s, James Kay, who came to run eighty-six public houses, set up his brewery here. There was also a James Kay brewery on Lower Hillgate, in Stockport, by the early 1950s.

Opposite, below: The Atlas Brewery building, used later by British Vinegars Ltd, on the east side of Stockport Road, *c.* 1958. It became part of Robinson's Brewery in 1929. Once its Gothic tower and chimney were a landmark on Stockport Road. In the 1960s the building was closed down, and was later demolished. (Courtesy of Manchester Archives and Local Studies at Central Library)

Above, left: A bottle for the ginger beer produced by James Dyson of Stockport Road, Longsight. He operated from the corner of Ducie Street and was active from the early 1900s. The brewers Slack & Cox Ltd also had their bottling plant at Ducie Street in the 1920s, with their manufactory in Ardwick. The spring water around east Manchester attracted mineral water manufacturers, such as Arthur Edge of Plymouth Grove, R.S. Holman of Longsight and Camwal Ltd of Stockport Road, Longsight.

Above, right: Edward Pemberton, founder of the Pemberton cycle-making firm, who lived from 1862 until 1930. In 1896 Edward founded the firm in Openshaw, on Ashton Old Road. As well as hand-made cycles, he produced crystal wireless sets with valves, installed in crafted cabinets. Later he moved the business to premises at Longsight, on Stockport Road between Longden Road and Matthews Lane.

Left: Edward Pemberton's shop on Stockport Road, Longsight, during the First World War. Edward's second wife, Sarah Ellen, ran the shop as a drapery during the war, as she was a dressmaker, while Edward, being involved in war work, could manage only cycle repairs. Their children stand outside the shop; from the left are: Marion (born in 1913), an unknown girl, Frank (born 1910) and his twin Madge.

Below: Fred Pemberton, Edward's son, building a bicycle frame in the workshop at their Longsight premises. Fred, his brothers Bernard and Albert, and sisters Kate and Nellie were born and brought up in Openshaw. The firm produced the famous Pemberton Arrow cycles, which were seen often at Fallowfield stadium, and where Fred himself raced. He was also made a life member of the Manchester Wheelers' Club.

Above: Pemberton's cycle shop after the First World War. Sarah Ellen died during childbirth in 1921. Edward changed his shop back to a cycle works, which later took in the shop next door. The shop signs proclaim: 'Cycles with real enamelling', 'Up to date battery charging' and the Pemberton Arrow motto: 'Promotes pride of possession'. In 1936 Fred moved with his family to a brand new shop in Sale, his son Harold joining him in 1944. Altogether the firm operated for eighty-eight years, making it Manchester's longest lasting cycle-makers.

Right: A billhead of 1923 for the family butcher's shop of Taylor Brothers on Stockport Road, Longsight. Matthias Taylor had been a butcher in Longsight in the 1870s and into the 1930s. Their wares included corn beef, pickled tongues and home-cured hams and bacons. Another butcher's shop and slaughterhouse was Wood's on Morton Street in Longsight, opposite a timber yard. James Wood had his butcher's shop as early as 1878 on Stockport Road.

Bill Nicholson standing outside a butcher's shop on Grey Street in 1958. Harold Sollinger had his butcher's shop near Rose View next to a greengrocery on Grey Street.

A letterhead of 1933 for the firm Robinson & Kershaw, constructional engineers and bridge builders. They had their main works in Ardwick at the Temple ironworks but their stockyard was in Longsight on Kirkmanshulme Lane.

Right: A *carte de visite* photograph showing a lady seated in a photographer's studio in the later 1800s. The photographer, F. Crowther, had his studio on Stockport Road, near one of the toll bars. These studio photographs were very popular, as few people owned their own camera until well into the 1900s.

Below: A map of the late 1800s showing Nutsford Vale, lying between Longsight and Gorton and home to various businesses. The Gore Brook, running through the vale, provided water for a chemical and dye works, plus an iron and a rope works. Earlier the vale was farmed at Catsknowl and Mount farms. Later, clay was extracted for brick making: J. & A. Jackson's Ltd, owned by Joseph Jackson, operated from Pink Bank Lane for fifty-two years and by marriage joined with Harrison's brick works of Levenshulme in 1922.

The headquarters of Jackson's brick works on Pink Bank Lane, Longsight. Later home to a private school, this head office was built by Thomas Warrington of Hyde and cost £5,702. The firm produced mainly common bricks. They opened other brick works, at places such as Cheadle, Denton and Audenshaw. They also had a shale-crushing plant at Longsight. When Christian Salvesen took them over in 1973, the Longsight premises were closed but sites such as Denton are still being used.

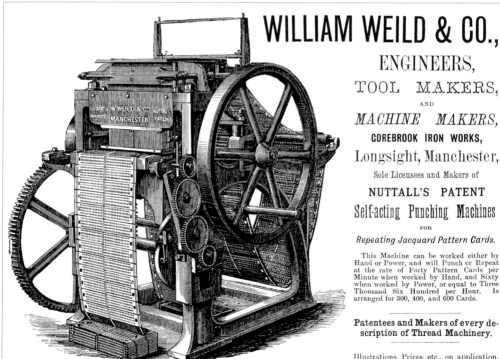

An advertisement of 1883 for the firm of William Weild & Co. of Gorebrook ironworks in Nutsford Vale. This engineering firm produced tools and machines off Pink Bank Lane. William became famous for his inventions: his automatic spooling machine won a prize medal at the Great Exhibition in London in 1862 and a gold medal at the Paris exhibition in 1867. His self-acting machines for the cotton industry made production less labour intensive and more efficient.

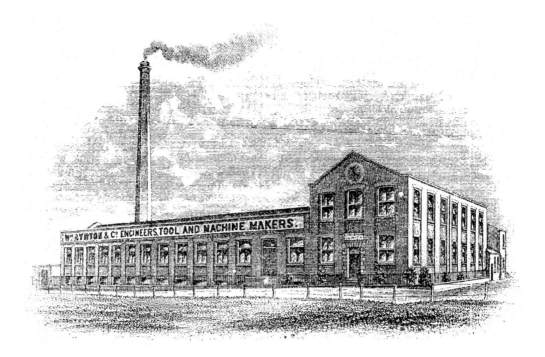

Above: A drawing of the purpose-built Gorebrook ironworks in 1892. William Ayrton took over the patents of the late William Weild and successfully produced his machinery. This included a self-acting spooling machine, which could wind six to eighteen spools simultaneously, the patent-improved Jacquard card-cutting machine, a card-lacing machine, repeating machines, Higgin's carding engines and a piano reading machine, plus oil cloth machinery.

Right: The new offices of the Gorebrook ironworks on Pink Bank Lane, bearing the foundation date of 1870. William Ayrton & Co. worked in this up-to-date purpose-built ironworks, where over a hundred workpeople provided specialist skills and were leaders in their field at home and abroad.

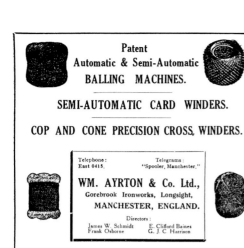

**Patent
Automatic & Semi-Automatic
BALLING MACHINES.**

SEMI-AUTOMATIC CARD WINDERS.

COP AND CONE PRECISION CROSS WINDERS.

Telephone: Telegrams :
East 0415.   "Spooler, Manchester."

WM. AYRTON & Co. Ltd.,
Gorebrook Ironworks, Longsight,
MANCHESTER, ENGLAND.

Directors :
James W. Schmidt   E. Clifford Baines
Frank Osborne   G. J. C Harrison

**Patent Automatic & Semi-Automatic
THREAD SPOOLING MACHINES.**

THREAD AND TWINE POLISHING MACHINES.

A world-wide Reputation for
Machinery of
Highest Efficiency & Durability
Since 1870.

Left: An advertisement of 1941 for William Ayrton & Co. in the *Cotton Year Book*. The list of their self-acting and semi-automatic machinery is impressive. William was himself a member of the Society of Arts. During the Second World War munitions were produced at the works.

Below: The daisy emblem in 1929 of W. & H. Pownall Ltd of Daisy Works Mill on Stockport Road. Pownall's were knitting and clothing manufacturers, as well as costume makers in their early days. In 1919 they also had a box-making department at the Thornville works next door. A bad fire in 1928 caused damage to the Daisy Works; it was repaired, enabling production to continue.

Pownall W. & H. Ltd.

Daisy works,
Stockport rd. Longsight
T N's 2,022 and 2,023
Central ;
T A " DAISIES "

The long frontage of the impressive five-storey Daisy Works Mill, on the north-east side of Stockport Road, with South Street running parallel behind it. The tall mill chimney has gone: it once boasted Pownall's name on it. Originally built as a textile mill occupied by Pownall's company, the building was used as an army pay corps office by the War Office during the Second World War. More recently it has been used by various small units such as a printer and a television dealer.

FIVE

ENTERTAINMENT AND LEISURE

Members of Longsight cycling club at Belle Vue stadium, where they held their annual races in the early 1900s.

Above: The King's Opera House on the north-west side of Stockport Road, *c.* 1915. It opened in 1904 as a theatre, presenting drama, comedy and vaudeville. It was part of the William H. Broadhead circuit: he married a Longsight girl called Ann Birch. Converted to a cinema in 1933 and run by the Shaftesbury Theatre Cinema Co., it closed in 1964 and was used as a club. The building, with its four purpose-built shops, was demolished in 1973. (Courtesy of Manchester Archives and Local Studies at Central Library)

Left: A programme, from about 1911, for the King's Theatre. Opposite it was the Shaftesbury Theatre, which lay between St John's and Church Roads. Opened in 1913, it was a cinema by 1919 and closed in May 1961. Like the King's, it was run by the Shaftesbury Cinema Theatre Co. Further along Stockport Road was the Queen's Picture Theatre opposite Slade Lane. Opened in 1914, it also became a cinema, and closed down in March 1961.

The Slade billiard hall at the top of Slade Lane by Slade Grove, near its junction with Stockport Road. On the right is the Beswick Society Co-operative building. The Slade Billiard Hall Co. Ltd operated this hall from the 1920s onwards. By the 1960s it was Riley's social and billiard club. More recently it has become a shop. (Courtesy of Manchester Archives and Local Studies at Central Library)

The Levenshulme Palais-de-Danse, *c.* 1959. Although named Levenshulme, this dance hall lay just near its border within Longsight, near Matthews Lane on Leeson Street. It was a modern, purpose-built ballroom, holding about 200–300 dancers and was very popular in the 1920s through to the early 1950s. (Courtesy of Manchester Archives and Local Studies at Central Library)

CAR PARK . BUFFET . RESIDENT ORCHESTRA
LARGEST SPRING FLOOR IN MANCHESTER

DANCING NIGHTLY

See daily details published in *Manchester Evening News* and
Evening Chronicle

General Manager: Bob Taylor   Telephone: RUSholme 2762

MANCHESTER'S famous BALLROOM de LUXE

Opposite, above: A 1948 advertisement for the Levenshulme Palais. Many people have fond memories of dancing here and of the various resident bands which provided the music. Later the building was used for roller skating, became the New Vaudeville Club in the 1970s, was used by the British Legion and finally became a mosque, until a fire in 2000 ended the building's use.

Opposite, below: Longsight cricket club, off East Road. Founded in 1848 at the George & Dragon public house in Ardwick, by 1922 the club had 320 full members. They also provided bowling, tennis, billiards and entertainment facilities. In 1878 the touring Australian cricket team played them with W.G. Grace on the English team. The club has played in the Lancashire & Cheshire League.

Members of the Longsight cycling club at Belle Vue in the early 1900s. That Saturday they held their annual races there, which included the One Mile Novice Handicap and the Twenty-Five Mile Championship. The latter was won by Herbert Watts in heavy rain and taking one hour, eighteen and a half minutes. Herbert was born in Rusholme, lived at Sunny Bank on Birch Hall Lane near Dickenson Road and was a keen cyclist.

The Longsight cycling club outside their club house after their races at Belle Vue, in the early 1900s. The One Mile Novice Handicap was won by F. Goldthorp by a length. A cycling club still exists on East Road in Longsight.

Opposite, above: Longsight Rovers football team, after winning the cup in the Manchester & District League at Ashton's Curzon ground in 1972. From left to right, back row: a coach, the manager Gordon Connolly, Ken Hampson, Alan Pentith, Dave Bowyer, Ken Hadley, Stuart Carr, Stan Bachelor and a coach. Front row: Ted Turner, Tommy Woods, Pete Dempsey, Tommy Barton, George Cannon,-?- and Stuart Williams.

Opposite, below: Longsight Rovers football team, school friends at Victoria Park Secondary School, in their 1967/8 season. From left to right, back row: Tommy Barton, Stan Bachelor, the captain Ken Hampson, George Cannon and goalkeeper Walter McWilliams. Front row: Kenneth Hadley, Dave Cooper, Pete Dempsey, Tommy Bell and Stuart Williams. They all lived in Longsight and played in the Saturday Morning League.

Opposite, above: Longsight Rovers football team receiving their winners' cup in the early 1970s.

Opposite, below: Girl Guides of the Longsight Methodist Church company with their company leaders in the late 1950s.

A group of Scouts at camp from the company at St Clement's Church, *c.* 1937. Two of them would not return from the Second World War.

Members of the St Cyprian's Anglican Church Lads' Brigade on a Whit Walk in 1961. First right is Fred Torr and first left is John Hunter.

Members of St Cyprian's Lads' Brigade on a Whit Walk in 1961. Front left is Fred Torr.

Right: Bill Nicholson standing in the doorway of the Richmond Inn public house in 1960. This stood on Morton Street near Marlow Street. It was demolished as part of the clearances on a Compulsory Purchase Order in 1972.

Below: The Waggon & Horses public house on Stockport Road on the corner of Birch Lane in 1910. Since about 1690, horse-drawn coaches from Manchester to London stopped here but part of the cellars and the mounting stone were all that had survived. Early on, John Clarke of Hulme provided the beer, followed by the Kay & Whittaker Brewery and then Wilson's Brewery from 1904. Sadly the pub was demolished in the early 2000s.

Opposite, above: The Farmers Arms Hotel on Stockport Road, nearly opposite the Midway House public house and Ivy Chapel. It had a bowling green and is a tall three-storeyed building.

Opposite, below: Joseph Lomas Frith and his wife Mary Elizabeth (Lizzie), *née* Jack, licensees of the Farmers Arms Hotel on Stockport Road. After marriage in 1913, they became licensees here from the mid 1920s. Lizzie died there in 1926. A plumber by trade, Joseph was a 'gentleman landlord', who rarely served behind the bar but had mainly Irish waiters and barmaids living in.

Ernest and Joan Smale with their children Ann and Michael in the garden of the Farmers Arms Hotel in 1947. Michael was born there in 1946. Joseph Frith became infirm and his eldest daughter Joan and family moved in and ran the pub for him. When Joseph died in 1945, they continued to run the pub. Harold Budge followed as landlord in the 1950s.

Above: Joan, Mary and Tom Frith. Joan would become licensee at the Farmers Arms Hotel and then at the Wilton Arms in Denton, when she was widowed. Mary was to hold the licence of the Bay Horse Inn in Longsight. Tom was to die in action in the RAF, aged only twenty-four, during the Second World War.

Left: The Bay Horse Inn on Stockport Road in 1974. It was a beer retailer's shop in the 1920s. Mrs Enid Burman was licensee in the 1940s and '50s. Another member of Joseph Frith's family at the Farmers Arms Hotel, Mary, who married William McKeown, was also licensee there. A butcher's shop on the right became an extension for the pub.

Right: Harold Hampson, landlord of the Bay Horse Inn with his dog 'Whiskey' in the backyard in the late 1960s. He remained landlord here until his death in 1972, when his wife Gladys took over running the pub.

Below: The Midway House public house on the corner of Matthews Lane and Stockport Road, in 1904. Right on the border with Levenshulme, this building dated back to at least the mid-1850s, when the area was still rural. In 1879 John Davidson was the landlord, with John Little there in 1904. There was a bowling green. The pub was rebuilt and became, as it looks today, an extensive building.

Levenshulme
Midway House.

C'est un autre carte postale de Levenshulme
John. E. Howard

Left: A wedding photograph of Diane Mercer-Brown and Kenneth Hampson, taken at their wedding reception in October 1968. They were married at St John's Church. They pose here on the stairway inside the Midway House public house.

Below: A bird's-eye view of Belle Vue Zoological Gardens in 1895. John Jennison acquired Belle Vue House and grounds on Hyde Road in 1836, moving in his small zoo. He gained thirteen more acres of farmland in 1843; by 1905 he had sixty-eight acres inside plus ninety-seven acres outside Belle Vue, within Longsight and Gorton. The Jennison family ran Belle Vue until 1925, when the Iles family, heading the Belle Vue (Manchester) Co. Ltd took over successfully. In 1956 the Forté family bought Belle Vue and concentrated more on its mass catering facilities.

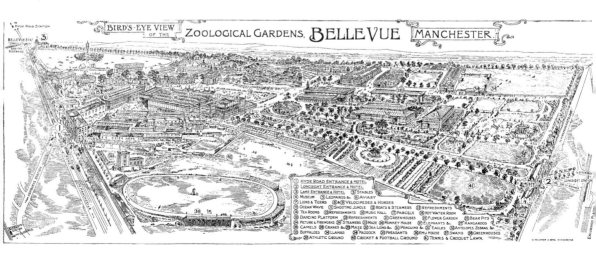

The Longsight entrance to Belle Vue Zoological Gardens, off Redgate Lane, west of Hunter's Lane, in 1909. John Jennison, who created this huge leisure park in 1836, was an astute businessman. Various gateways brought visitors in easily and quickly from both Gorton and Longsight. This was the western gateway and lay near Longsight station, which had room for the excursion trains for Belle Vue.

The Longsight entrance to Belle Vue in its final days. Costing £1,000 when built in 1851, it housed a ballroom in its upper storey. A long tree-lined avenue led visitors through landscaped gardens to the attractions. By the 1950s the top storey was demolished. The entrance, plus the Longsight Hotel (originally part of this entrance), was pulled down when Belle Vue closed. A new Longsight Inn was built on Kirkmanshulme Lane.

Opposite above, left: An advertisement of 1948 for Belle Vue. John Jennison certainly created the 'showground of the world', a theme park before such attractions became fashionable.

Opposite above, right: An advertisement of 1974 for Belle Vue. Everything that a visitor needed was provided within the walls of Belle Vue: beautiful gardens, a zoo, amusement parks, lakes, music, dancing and firework displays. Catering served everyone, from banquets to picnics and ice-cream, and from beer to ginger beer, all produced in the grounds. Later, a miniature railway, exhibition and banqueting halls were added.

Opposite, below: Belle Vue gardens, near the Longsight entrance in 1905. Here the area for the fountain and District House (formerly the Emu House) is adorned by sculpture and flower beds. The gardens were vast and covered quite an area of the Longsight section of Belle Vue including, from 1853 onwards, long tree-lined avenues to link the gardens with the Longsight entrance and Longsight station on Kirkmanshulme Lane.

The Italian gardens at Belle Vue in 1938. Each area was themed, such as the Indian temple and grotto and these gardens, which were laid out in 1870 by George Jennison (John's son). They included tropical plant houses and other glasshouses, where flowers, fruit and vegetables were grown for use in decorating the buildings and in catering.

The Indian temple and grotto at Belle Vue in 1928. A monkey house was built in an Indian style in 1886 and these grottoes followed in 1898. The 'ruined Indian temple' style was designed by George Danson, who was part of the family of scenic artists who designed the firework backdrops each year.

Another view of the Indian temple and grotto rockery in 1956.

The pelican enclosure at Belle Vue in the late 1950s. Bill Brown sits on the wall. Originally the pelicans were in the indoor Birds of Prey Terrace, gazed at by visitors from a viewing gallery. By the 1930s they had their own enclosure. In 1959 the Birdcage Walk was created from the old Monkey Terrace: the old Birds of Prey Terrace was replaced in 1962 with a second Birdcage Walk. Visitors could view the pelicans at their tea-time feeding session.

The giraffes at Belle Vue in 1956. A small giraffe house was built originally on Paddock Range. Initially there were few successes with breeding them, until Gerald Iles became Zoo Director in the 1930s. Giraffes such as George, Willie, Mary and Doreen were popular with the visitors.

Having fun in the amusement park at Belle Vue in the mid-1960s. The Jennisons had a small area set out with steam-driven attractions in the 1870s, just east of the main Hyde Road entrance. In the 1920s, John Henry Iles set out a new amusement park, west of the main Hyde Road gateway, and an area for small children followed in 1931. The 'Bobs' rollercoaster and the scenic railway rides were probably the most famous of all the amusements.

Dismantling the Longsight entrance in 1981. Changing attitudes meant fewer visitors. Fires, vandalism and theft were serious problems by the late 1960s. The zoo closed in 1977; in 1981 most of Belle Vue was sold for housing and commercial use. Only the greyhound/speedway stadium outside the site survives. The closure impacted on Longsight and Gorton with a loss of jobs and visitors and the closure of some local public houses and other amenities.

SIX

EVENTS

The younger members of the church take part in a May Day procession along Stockport Road in the 1920s. The girl at the back on the right carries a placard announcing 'SPRING' and the retinue attends the queen. Watching on the right is Mary Shaw.

New fuselage for the Avro 618, in transit from the Avro Newton Heath factory via Longsight, for reassembly at Avro at the company's Woodford works in 1933. Built at Newton Heath for the Australian National Airways in 1929 and christened *Southern Moon*, it flew the first Melbourne to Sydney service in 1930. Later, purchased by Charles Ulm and rechristened *Faith in Australia*, it began a world flight but, in 1933, became partially submerged near Dublin. So this new fuselage was made. The plane broke various records and, when the Japanese entered the Second World War, it evacuated personnel until its final journey from Horn Island in 1942, before finally being scrapped in late 1944.

A family in Ernest Street ready for the Whit Sunday Walks in 1954. The street lay just north of Richmond Street East. From the left stand Bill, Diane and Steve Brown in their best clothes. Behind them is New Bank Street, running from Hyde Road up to Kirkmanshulme Lane. Beyond New Bank Street run the railway lines for Longsight sidings.

Right: The same trio ready for the Whit Sunday Walks six years later in 1960. By then they were living on East Road, just north of Crowcroft Park. From left to right stand Bill, Diane and Steve Brown.

Below: Bill and Alice Nicholson wait behind four of their children, James, Billy, Pat and John, and family friend Rodney Garner, for the start of the Whit Walks, *c.* 1960. They are standing outside St Clement's Church.

Above: Beryl Nicholson with her sister Pat on the left, ready for the Whit Walk in 1956. They are standing on New Bank Street and walked with St Clement's Church.

Left: John Nicholson, their brother, walking on New Bank Street in 1960, as part of the Whit Walk procession with St Clement's Church.

Above: Members of the children's section take part in a Whit Walk in the mid-1940s. They are negotiating the tram lines along Stockport Road. Their banners proclaim 'Jesus Leads Us On' and 'Sunbeams for Him'. Ann Atkinson (*née* Smale) is the young girl second from the right.

Right: Another Whit Walk procession makes its way along Stockport Road in 1948. Members of the Sunday school lead the way.

Opposite, above: Beryl Nicholson, on the left, taking part in a Whit Walk, *c.* 1954. She is with members of St Clement's Church on Morton Street.

Opposite, below: Two views of Whit Walks in the late 1940s.

Members of North Road Methodist Church make their way along North (later Northmoor) Road, *c.* 1957. The placard top left proclaims: 'We save. Just welcomed new members. How About You?' First front left is Bill Brown and his brother Steve is first front right. They have turned from East Road into North Road with Crowcroft Park behind them.

Right: Boys of Longsight Methodist Church carry their banner in the Whit Walks along Stockport Road in the early 1950s.

Left: Some children of Longsight Methodist Church process along Stockport Road in a Whit Walk in the early 1950s.

Below: Younger members of St Cyprian's Anglican Church in a Whit Walk procession, *c.* 1957. Gwynne Brindley is first on the right.

Above: Members of St Cyprian's Anglican Church make their way along North (later Northmoor) Road, *c*. 1957. They are just passing the North Road Beswick Co-operative Society building. Third from the left is Gwynne Brindley, holding one of the banner ribbons.

Right: Christine Kinsey, Rose Queen of Longsight Methodist Church, leads her retinue along Earl Street on the Whit Walk in 1957. The shop on the left advertises its wares as 'Cornbrook Ales and Stouts' and 'Capstan' cigarettes. Earl Street lay parallel to, and just east of, Stockport Road.

Rose Queen Christine Kinsey poses with the Rose Bud Queen on the steps of Longsight Methodist Church with their attendants in 1957. Among them are sisters Susan and Sally Kinsey.

Rodney Garner (far left) and John Nicholson (far right) escort the cross bearer of St Clement's Church along Morton Street on the Whit Walk in 1960.

Christine Kinsey, that year's Rose Queen, lined up with her retinue for the Whit Walks in 1957. They are outside Longsight Methodist Church on Stockport Road.

The Rose Bud, with all her attendants, poses on the steps of Longsight Methodist Church in the early 1950s.

Opposite, above: Gwynne Brindley playing on her bike in her back yard at home on Link Street. The year is 1953 and the Union Jack flag celebrates the Coronation of Elizabeth II after her accession to the throne in 1952.

Opposite, below: A street party to celebrate the Coronation of Queen Elizabeth II in 1953. This one was for the neighbours of Morton and Ernest Streets. The children seated from left to right are Steve, Bill and Diane Brown with their grandmother Mary Shaw standing behind Diane.

Above: The Longsight National Savings Queens for the years 1945–7. This encouraged savers in the Longsight Saving Group. The retiring queen, together with the new queen, is surrounded by their attendants and behind them are held standards topped by the National Savings emblem.

Left: Celebrating a special day with a street party, photographed by Bertram Boor, a Longsight photographer, in the 1920s. In the centre sits Kastain, who succeeded George Danson as scenic artist and designer at Belle Vue Zoological Gardens.

SEVEN

AT CHURCH
AND SCHOOL

Mrs Haywood with her class of 1960/61 at Crowcroft Park Primary School. This county primary school was opened on North (later Northmoor) Road in 1935 to serve the surrounding terraced housing. Although on the border with Levenshulme in the ward of Gorton South, most of its pupils have come from Longsight.

The interior of St John's Anglican Church in 1914. Dedicated to St John the Apostle and Evangelist, it was consecrated in 1846, making it Longsight's earliest Anglican church. The cost of £4,000 was raised mainly by subscription and from a donation by the Marshall family of Ardwick House. The site was given by Sir J.W.H. Anson. There was seating for 950 people: 400 of these were free places.

The wedding of Diane Mercer-Brown and Kenneth Hampson in October 1968. They were married in St John's Anglican Church and are pictured here leaving the altar.

St. John's Church, Longsight, Manchester.

Above: The exterior of St John's Anglican Church in the 1920s. The building lies between Holmfirth Street and St John's Road. The architect of this early English-style church was John Edgar Gregan. It was the only Longsight Anglican church with a graveyard, but burials ceased in 1966. In 1979 St John's amalgamated with St Cyprian's, Longsight. Finally the two churches became united with St Agnes; St John's building became disused and was sold.

Right: The wedding of Beryl Nicholson and Tony Williams in 1963. They were married in St John's Church and are seen here just leaving the altar.

St John's Church School. The school was opened in 1831 with additions in the 1960s. Fires caused the school to be rebuilt in 1990 and it is now on Clarence Road. (Courtesy of Manchester Archives and Local Studies at Central Library)

The exterior of St Agnes's Anglican Church in 1915. Lying between Slade Lane and Hamilton Road, this fine, brick church, designed by brothers Henry and Medland Taylor, was consecrated in 1885 on land given by Sir W.R. Anson. The name of Agnes came from the names of the wives of Bishop Fraser and Archdeacon Anson, both supporters of its establishment.

The rectory of St Agnes's Anglican Church on Slade Lane. This house is in keeping with the style of the church. Medland Taylor designed many rectories to accompany his churches around Manchester, including two at Denton and one at Ashton-under-Lyne. In 1997 the three churches of St John, St Cyprian and St Agnes were amalgamated, with St Agnes continuing in use.

The demolition of the Church of England primary school of St Agnes in 2008. This school, on the corner of Hamilton and Clitheroe Roads, was opened in 1885 on land given by the Anson family. The building was extended again and again to accommodate increasing numbers. Tennis and netball took place in Birch Fields Park, and woodwork at Stanley Grove Primary School. St Agnes's Primary School is now the first in Britain to be rebuilt from a flat-pack, using pre-fabricated wooden frames made in Switzerland.

Left: The baptism certificate of Peter Ford in 1936. He was baptised at St Clement's Anglican Church in December of that year.

Below: The church schools of St Clement's Anglican Church on Dillon Street. The school was originally opened as Grey Street School for nearby St Matthew's Anglican Church in Ardwick. When the parish of St Clement (consecrated in 1876) was formed, the school changed its name. The church and schools were all designed by Medland Taylor. A new school building was opened in 1970. The church closed in 1974 and was demolished. (Courtesy of Manchester Archives and Local Studies at Central Library)

An early view of the interior of St Robert's Roman Catholic Church. A few worshippers kneel before the Forty Hours Exposition on the altar. This church was opened in 1915 but was replaced later by a larger, more modern building. The church lay near Hamilton Road and Slade Lane between Farrer and Montgomery Roads. It was closed down in around 2003 and was later demolished.

An early view of the interior of St Joseph's Roman Catholic Church on Plymouth Grove. The original chapel was in St Joseph's Technical School on Plymouth Grove from 1888. Then this church was opened in 1915 by the Lord Mayor of Dublin: it was not consecrated until 1988. The Little Sisters of the Poor have their home opposite the church and they and the Opus Dei Prelature worship at St Joseph's Church. The presbytery has been on Portland Crescent for a while.

The former St Joseph's Industrial School for boys, 1958. Situated on the west side of Stockport Road, it was opened in 1870 and included a chapel. Taken over by Manchester Education authority, it was later used by the auxiliary fire service during the Second World War and continued as their training college. By 1958, Manchester City Police was using it as a divisional headquarters, transport depot and hostel, until demolition when a new police station opened in 1998. (Courtesy of Manchester Archives and Local Studies at Central Library)

North (later Northmoor) Road Wesleyan Methodist Chapel in 1925. Inset is the minister Revd H. Powell. This combined school/chapel was opened on the corner of East and North Roads in 1911 at a cost of £1,633. In 1959 a new church building was opened and the former church became solely a school; now it is a nursery. The church changed its name to Northmoor in 1968 to match the new road name.

Right: An early view of Longsight Wesleyan Methodist Chapel on Stockport Road. After meeting in various cottages from 1816 onwards, the original church/ school was built near Richmond Grove East. This is the second church that replaced it in 1869 and would become neighbour to Daisy Works Mill.

Below: Longsight Wesleyan Methodist Chapel in 1889. Their former church building is visible further up the road. The increasing congregation opened this larger, Gothic style church in 1869, to a design by William Hayley at a cost of £8,000. By 1966 a new church and community centre were built next door, but closed in 1986.

LONGSIGHT WESLEYAN CHAPEL.

H.E.T.

LONGSIGHT WESLEYAN... ...SUNDAY SCHOOL.

MOTTO for 1908:
"Be not weary in well doing."—*2 Thess. iii. 13.*

DEAR FRIEND,

The Officers and Teachers heartily Congratulate you on your Birthday, and earnestly pray that you may have many prosperous years, with all spiritual joy and happiness.

Miss *Fanny Gregory*

Dec 13 1908

A birthday card sent by Longsight Wesleyan Methodist Sunday school in December 1908. It was sent to Fanny Gregory and there is a prayer on the reverse side of the card.

The datestone of 1893 on the Sunday school building of the College Chapel Methodist Free Church on Hamilton Road. The students from Victoria Park College opened this as their chapel until the new, larger one was built for them next door in 1907. This 1893 building is now used as a community centre by the Church of God of Prophecy.

The former Victoria Park Methodist College Chapel on the corner of Hamilton and Dickenson Roads in 2006. Opened in 1907 as a larger chapel for students at Victoria Park College, it was known as the United Methodist Free Church. The college closed down in 1934 but the church continued until 1978. It has reopened as the Church of God of Prophecy. On the left is the building of the former printing works of the Co-operative Wholesale Society Ltd.

Longsight Presbyterian Church on Stockport Road and Richmond Grove East (left) in the 1950s. It was opened in 1870 in a building originally erected by the Longsight Wesleyan Methodist Church. A Sunday school was added in 1873. A theatre group, the Longsight Players, used the church hall. The church closed in the late 1960s and was demolished during redevelopment of the area. (Courtesy of Manchester Archives and Local Studies at Central Library)

The Longsight Free Christian Church, on the corner of Birch Lane (on the left) and Plymouth Grove, in the 1930s or '40s. Elizabeth Gaskell's husband, Revd William Gaskell, laid one of the foundation stones in 1882.

The Longsight Free Christian Church in the 1940s. This elegant tower was removed after lightning damage. In 1948 the church closed due to falling numbers. The BBC used the building as a van depot; it became a warehouse in the 1980s and was eventually demolished.

The 1929 foundation stone of the Longsight Baptist Church Sunday school building. This lies next to the church on Slade Lane on the corner of Palm Street. This was also a First World War Memorial. By 1910 the Sunday school had increased to 213 children and so there was a need for this building in 1929. The Church of God Seventh Day now uses the church building.

The Longsight Baptist Church Sunday school in 1929, and the memorial foundation stone of 1898, over the entrance to Longsight Baptist church. This replaced the 'Tin Tabernacle', an iron building which the Baptists opened on the corner of Slade Lane and Slade Grove in 1887. Opened in 1900, the church had 118 members by 1910 and had been able to build a mission church elsewhere in Longsight in 1902.

BAPTIST COLLEGE MISSION, LONGSIGHT

Above: The Baptist College Mission Hall on Halsbury Street in the early 1900s. This was opened by the Baptists in 1902 to serve the mass of people in the terraced housing in that area. The foundation stone reads, '1902. C.H.H. Cast Thy Burden on the Lord.' (Courtesy of Manchester Archives and Local Studies at Central Library)

Left: A certificate presented by the Earl Street Mission branch of the Manchester City Mission in 1948. This attractive document contains a small picture of the mission hall. The certificate was presented for long service to Mr and Mrs R.J. Dupre and contains the names of the mission council and organist. The hall lay amid terraced housing at the top of South Street near Richmond Grove. It was demolished in the late 1960s during the redevelopment of the area.

Above, left: Pastor John Nelson Parr, who opened the Bethshan Tabernacle on Crowcroft Road in 1928. Born in Ardwick in 1886, he was co-founder of the Assemblies of God of Great Britain and Ireland Pentecostalism revolution.

Above, right: Pastor John Nelson Parr cutting a cake to celebrate the opening of the Bethshan Tabernacle in 1928. The cake is a small replica of the tabernacle. With a congregation of 400, it became one of the largest in the country. The church is now renamed the Bethshan International Church.

Right: An early view of the Independent Chapel on Lime Grove, off Stockport Road, next to the fire station. Opened in 1853 and with its ivy-covered front wall known as the Ivy Chapel, it became Longsight's fashionable church. Designed by Travis and Mangnall at a cost of £5,000, it included Sunday school infants' rooms and a chapel keeper's house. It closed in 1933 as numbers dwindled, was leased as a fun fair centre and was finally demolished during the 1960s for re-housing schemes.

Left: The home of the Reorganised Church of the Latter Day Saints on Beresford Road in 2008. Originally they met in a coal yard in Mundy Street near Stockport Road and Stanley Grove. This church was opened in 1923 by evangelist Richard Baldwin, accompanied by a procession of 200 members and friends. The Community of Christ still uses this building.

Below: A certificate awarded to Pat Nicholson for her excellent attendance at Plymouth Grove Primary School for the school year 1959/60. Situated on the south side of Plymouth Grove West, this red brick, three-storied building was opened in 1906 as the forty-third School of Manchester Education Committee for infants through to senior pupils.

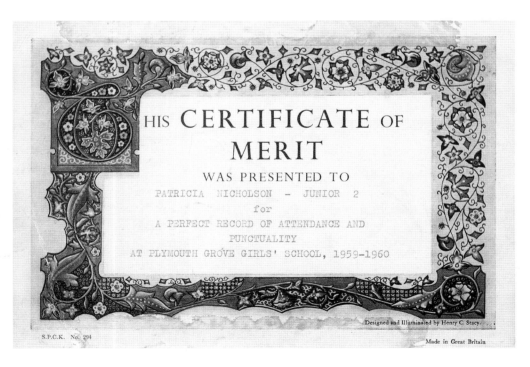

HIS **CERTIFICATE** OF **MERIT**

WAS PRESENTED TO

PATRICIA NICHOLSON – JUNIOR 2

for

A PERFECT RECORD OF ATTENDANCE AND PUNCTUALITY

AT PLYMOUTH GROVE GIRLS' SCHOOL, 1959-1960

Designed and Illuminated by Henry C. Stacy.

S.P.C.K. No. 294

Made in Great Britain

Right: The memorial stone on the front wall of Stanley Grove School. The school was founded on Stanley Grove by the Manchester School Board in 1902 and handed over to the new Manchester Education Committee the following year. In 1998 the infant and junior departments were amalgamated.

Below: An early class photograph of boys only, at Stanley Grove School. The school served the people living in the terraced housing around it. It would become a community school and include a nursery.

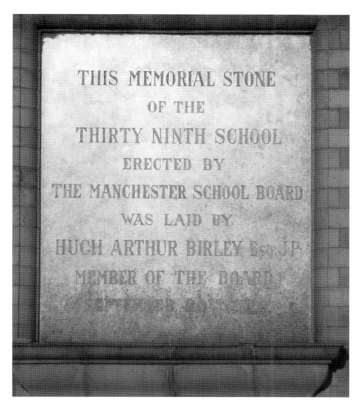

THIS MEMORIAL STONE
OF THE
THIRTY NINTH SCHOOL
ERECTED BY
THE MANCHESTER SCHOOL BOARD
WAS LAID BY
HUGH ARTHUR BIRLEY Esq. J.P.
MEMBER OF THE BOARD

A class photo of pupils at Stanley Grove Primary School, *c.* 1963. Third row from the front, fifth from the left, is Gillian Brindley. The late actor John Thaw was also a past pupil.

A class, with their teacher Miss Greenhalgh, at Crowcroft Park primary school in 1959. From left to right, back row: -?-, -?-, -?-, Grace Baskerfield, Jacqueline ?, Dorothea Beddows, -?-, -?-, Elizabeth Matthews, -?-, Jane Tyrrell, Jean Read. Second row from the back: -?-, -?-, David Bailey, Clive -?-, Eric Botham, Brian Anderson, -?-, -?-, -?-, -?-, -?-. Third row from back: Sandra Day, -?-, Susan Birch, -?-, Frances ?, Diane Brown, -?-, -?-, Ruth Whittaker, Linda Simpkin. Front row: -?-, Lance Williams, -?-, -?-, Stuart Sykes, -?-, -?-.

A postcard used to send season's greetings from Mr and Mrs John Guard of No. 88 Albert Grove, Longsight. The card has been reused in 1910 to send a message between the Marsh family.

WE MISS
THE PATTER
OF YOUR
LITTLE FEET
IN LONGSIGHT

A humorous postcard sent from Longsight to Lancaster in 1912 by a daughter wishing her mother better.

Other titles published by The History Press

Clayton and Openshaw
JILL CRONIN AND FRANK RHODES

Clayton and Openshaw are districts of East Manchester that, over a century and a half, have experienced a sequence of industrial growth followed by recession, massive clearances and redevelopment. These fascinating old photographs show town and rural scenes, buildings, people at work and leisure and have been collected from a variety of local sources including the family albums of people who grew up there. The book is a source of nostalgia for those who remember the towns in their heyday.

978 0 7524 3521 3

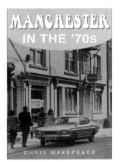

Manchester in the '70s
CHRIS MAKEPEACE

Featured here along with street scenes of the city centre and suburbs are images of people, buildings, transport, events and a number of sites which have changed beyond recognition. Most of the photographs included in this book were taken by the author and have never been published before. They are supplemented by posters and adverts to capture the true flavour of the decade. *Manchester in the '70s* is sure to stir feelings of nostalgia in anyone who lived or worked in the city during this fascinating decade.

978 0 7509 4615 5

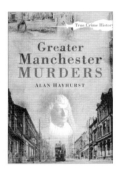

Greater Manchester Murders
ALAN HAYHURST

Contained within the pages of this book are the stories behind some of the most notorious murders in the history of Greater Manchester. They include the case of cat burglar Charlie Peace, who killed a young policeman in Seymour Grove, and only confessed after he had been sentenced to death for another murder; John Jackson, who escaped from Strangeways Gaol after killing a prison warder; and the death of Police Sergeant Charles Brett, who stuck bravely to his post despite an armed attack on his prison van by the 'Manchester Martyrs'.

978 0 7509 5091 6

Hanged at Manchester
STEVE FIELDING

For decades the high walls of Manchester's Strangeways Prison have contained some of England's most infamous criminals. They include Dr Buck Ruxton, who butchered his wife and maid; Walter Rowland, hanged for the murder of a prostitute; and Oldham teenager Ernie Kelly, whose execution almost caused a riot outside the prison. Also included are the stories behind scores of lesser-known criminals: poisoners, spurned lovers, cut-throat killers, and many more.

978 0 7509 5052 7

Visit our website and discover thousands of other History Press books.

www.thehistorypress.co.uk